S0-FQV-750

# PRACTICAL *philanthropy*

## How 'Giving Back' Helps You, Your Business, and the World Around You

# LAURA ORSINI

*Practical Philanthropy: How 'Giving Back' Helps You, Your Business, and the World Around You*

Copyright © 2014 Moondanz Creationz All rights reserved.

All rights reserved, including the right of reproduction in whole or in part of any form. No part of this book may be used to reproduce by any means, graphic, electronic, or mechanical, including photocopying, recording, taping, or by any information storage retrieval system without the written permission of the author except in the case of brief quotations embodied in critical articles and reviews.

ISBN 978-0-9904056-0-3

Printed in the United States

This book is available at quantity discounts for both purchases and for branding by businesses and organizations. For further information about *Practical Philanthropy* or Moondanz Creationz, please inquire, as indicated:

Moondanz Creationz
PO Box 40273
Phoenix, AZ 85067

602.518.5376
info@MoondanzCreationz.com
MoondanzCreationzcom

Cover design by Laura Orsini
Illustrations by Laura Orsini
Page composition and typography by Laura Orsini

# DEDICATION

for John

# ACKNOWLEDGEMENTS

This book began as a presentation for the Your Vibrant Business virtual summit, created by my friend, Karen Gridley, a business coach and speaker. The subject has long been near and dear to my heart, and I appreciated the platform and opportunity to share this information.

Given the time boundaries allowed for the virtual summit presentation, I was forced to limit the contents. This book gave me the room to flesh out my ideas a bit and incorporate a bit of art to inspire my readers.

Thanks go out to my mom and dad, now deceased, wherever they may be. I will be forever grateful for the lessons in compassion and altruism they instilled in me.

May the lessons they taught me similarly inspire you.

# CONTENTS

Understanding the Terms ................................... 1

Paving the Way to Become a Giver ................................... 7

What's in It for Me? ................................... 17

Can One Person Really Make a Difference? ................................... 33

Where Should I Begin? ................................... 45

Ways to Give Back ................................... 53

Be Sure to Toot Your Own Horn ................................... 77

Thoughts for the "Overgivers" ................................... 85

Share Your Ideas & Success Stories! ................................... 101

Notes ................................... 105

Art 4 the Homeless & Saint Vincent de Paul ................................... 111

About the Author ................................... 115

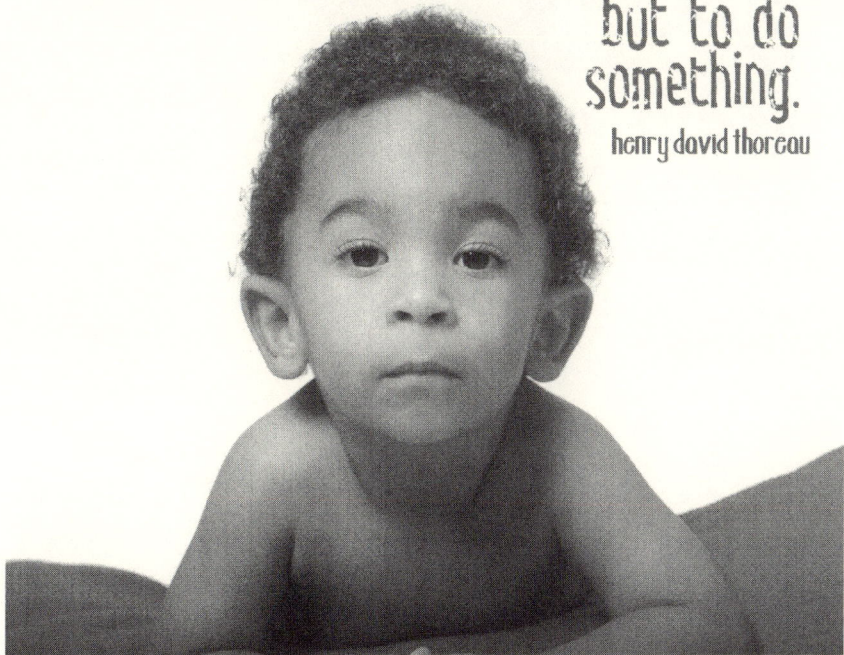

One is not born
into the world to do everything,

but to do
something.

henry david thoreau

*chapter 1*

# Understanding the Terms

"Practical philanthropy" is not a new term. On Google Books, you can find an electronic version of the book, *A Lesson in Practical Philanthropy: Dr. D.K. Pearson's Method of Helping Poor Colleges.*[1] The original book was the printed version of the October 1898 address delivered by Daniel Kimball Pearsons to the Civic-Philanthropic Conference in Battle Creek, Michigan.

Nearly eighty years old when he gave his address, Dr. Kimball began:

> I shall talk to you to-night in plain language. I am about to say some things I have never before mentioned in the presence of an audience. In other words, I propose to be very frank, very plain. My subject is: "What to Do with Money — How to Use It."

Clearly, Dr. Kimball had a different understanding of the term "practical philanthropy" than I will apply to the subject. Let's begin by looking at a few definitions:

> **PRACTICAL:** relating to what is real, rather than to what is possible or imagined; likely to succeed and reasonable to do or use; appropriate or suited for actual use

**PHILANTHROPY,** *etymologically*: "love of humanity" in the sense of caring for, nourishing, developing, and enhancing the things that make us human, on behalf of both the benefactors and beneficiaries; *contemporary use*: the desire to promote the welfare of others, expressed especially by the generous donation of money to good causes

The word *philanthropy* was first used by the playwright Aeschylus in *Prometheus Bound* to describe Prometheus as "humanity loving" for giving fire and optimism to the earliest humans, who had before that been without culture. Together, these things would improve the human condition and save mankind from destruction. Thus humans were set apart from all other animals by civilization, self-development, and culture, expressed through good works that benefit others.[2]

Given that there is no "official" definition of practical philanthropy, here's the definition I offer:

**PRACTICAL PHILANTHROPY:** making a difference in a way that is reasonable and *doable* for your life

Traditional philanthropy can tend to be distant and impersonal, people doing good without really getting involved or even getting to know their beneficiaries. One thing about practical philanthropy is the opportunity it offers to interact with the people you're helping.

# Review Question

How do *you* define *practical philanthropy*?

_____

_____

_____

_____

_____

IN A GENTLE
WAY, YOU
CAN SHAKE
THE WORLD.
MAHATMA GANDHI

*chapter 2*

# Paving the Way to Become a Giver

For some of us, giving comes more naturally than it does for others. I grew up with parents who taught me to be a "giver," and as a result, giving is a part of who I am — to do otherwise would seem foreign to me. I remember noticing, as a little girl, some of the small things I did that other people — grown up people — didn't necessarily do, like hold the door open for the person behind me, or even saying "please" and "thank you." Like I said, I had good role models.

Before I share a couple stories from my childhood with you, let me make the caveat that these are my stories, my opinions, my ideas. You may agree with all of them, some of them, or none of them. My goal is simply to expose you to a new way of thinking or to reinvigorate a passion that may have gone dormant. Use what works for you — discard the rest.

I grew up in a Catholic household, and back then BINGO was less associated with Indian casinos than it was with Catholic parishes, which used the money generated by weekly BINGO games to defray expenses. My dad was instrumental in bringing BINGO to our parish, and he helped run the game for more than a dozen years. This particular incident must have been early in that run, as I was fairly young, perhaps 9 or 10 at the time.

My dad was away for his weekly BINGO outing, so my mom, my sister, and I were home on our own. It was the *only* night of the week my father ever went out — and as fortune would have it, it was the same night that a skinny, old (to me) man in a black trench coat rang our doorbell. I think back now to how desperate he must have been to approach the house of total strangers. Today, you might never open the door to an odd-looking visitor, but this was a different time and we answered the door.

The man explained to my mother that he was hungry and he hoped she might be able to offer him a sandwich or some other food to get him through the night. Instead of making a sandwich and sending him on his way — which I remember thinking would have been very generous of her — she invited the stranger into our house, sat him in my dad's chair at the dining room table, and fed him hot soup and *two* sandwiches. My sister and I stared, open-mouthed and wide-eyed, as the stranger gobbled up the food. I wondered how long it had been since he'd eaten, and why food seemed so hard for him to come by. Before sending him on his way, my mom packed the man a brown bag with a few more sandwiches.

Did my mom solve all the man's problems? Of course not. Did she expose us to potential danger by letting a stranger into the house? Perhaps. But the most important thing she did was teach me a lifelong lesson about giving. We had food — he didn't. He asked us for help and we were in a position to help

— so we helped. Period. While I don't remember her exact words, the gist of my mom's message was this: *When someone asks you for help and you are able, you help. If you give them money and they spend it on booze or do something else imprudent with it — that's between them and God. If they ask you for help and you don't help — that's between you and God.*

A few years later, my father had become involved with the Society of St. Vincent de Paul, whose mission is to serve the needy and the suffering. One of the most visible ways they do this is through their thrift stores and food pantries. Many Catholic parishes had St. Vincent de Paul leagues, made up of volunteers who worked to staff the parish food pantry and accept food requests from families inside the parish's geographic boundaries. These were not necessarily people who attended the church — just folks who lived nearby and knew the church as a resource if they were down on their luck.

Our parish had an active St. Vincent de Paul league, and my dad was its number one volunteer. Every Saturday like clockwork, he'd go on visits to deliver food boxes to those needy families. I'm not quite sure how it came about, but for a year or so, I accompanied my dad on these visits. Talk about eye-opening! Our family was not by any means wealthy, but even when my father was out of work for six months, he made sure that we never wanted for anything. So it was an incredibly enlightening and empathy-building experience to go into homes where the children were lucky to have a single pair of shoes and the babies were often naked because diapers were just too expensive.

My father passed away in 2005. After the funeral, we had a meal for friends and family in the parish hall — original home to the BINGO game he had instituted all those years ago. There was a lot of food left over, so my brother-in-law, following in my father's footsteps, suggested that we take the extra food to a downtown park where many of the city's homeless often congregate. There we were, David in his tuxedo, my sister and I in our best dresses, serving food out of the back of a rented SUV. I'll never forget one man who came up and asked for an extra piece of cake. "Sure! Why not?" we said. Our goal was just to give all the food away. I couldn't help but tear up as I watched the man proceed to break the cake into small pieces and share it with the birds. This man who had nothing made a deliberate effort to share what little we gave him. It was the perfect way to pay tribute to my dad's memory.

Though my father died long before the election of Pope Francis, he would have been overjoyed to see it. I imagine him celebrating from wherever he is right now, thrilled at the thought of a pope who prioritizes the needs of the poor the same way Jesus did.

So these experiences with each of my parents were among the events that shaped my childhood and led me to become the person — and business owner — I am today. Perhaps you had similar experiences, but more likely you did not. According to the U.S. Bureau of Labor Statistics, about 64.5 million American adults (26.5 percent) volunteered through or for an organization at least once in 2012. That number is down 0.3 percent since 2011, but has hovered in that range for the last 20 years or so. As might be expected, people are most likely to volunteer for or through a religious organization, followed by educational/youth service-related organizations, and then by social or community service organizations.[3]

So if 26.5 percent of American adults are giving back through volunteering, nearly three-quarters are not. The "why" is irrelevant. Like leadership or sales or mindset or marketing, I believe the "giving muscle" needs to be exercised regularly if it is to develop properly. If you haven't exercised yours in a while, it's never too late to start.

# Review Question

On a scale of 1 to 10 (10 being the highest), how would you rank your desire to incorporate "giving back" into your business model?

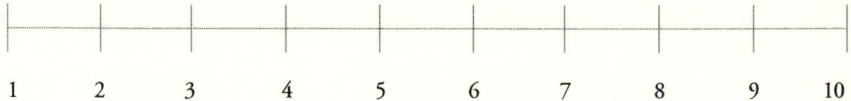

| | | | | | | | | | |
|---|---|---|---|---|---|---|---|---|---|
| 1 | 2 | 3 | 4 | 5 | 6 | 7 | 8 | 9 | 10 |

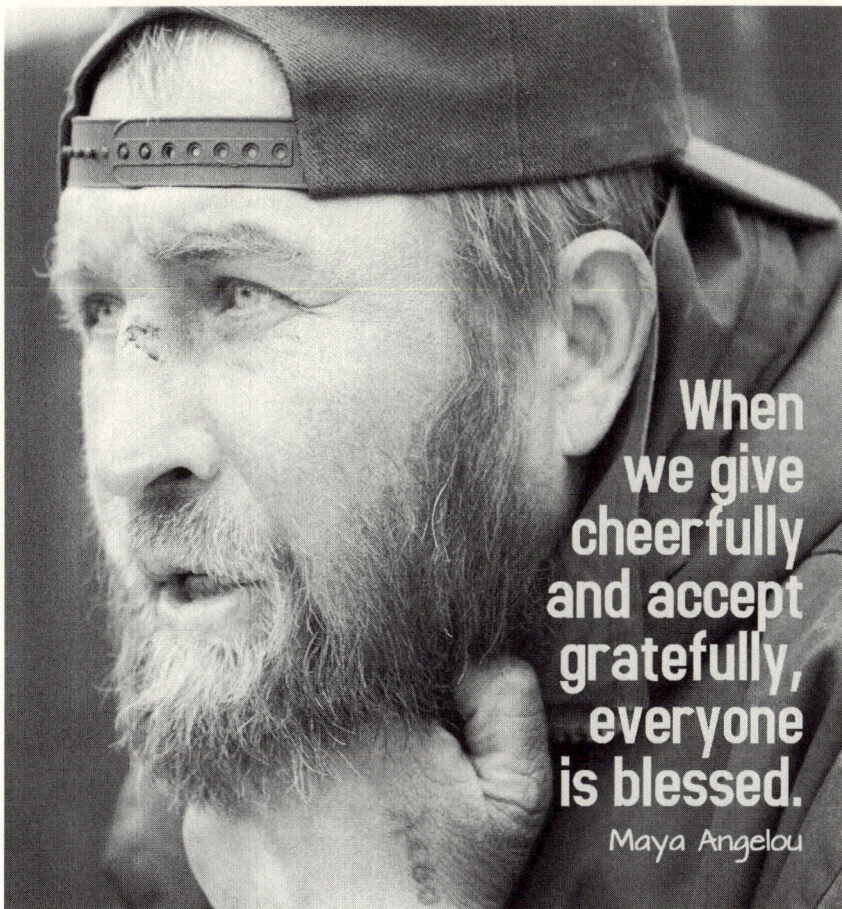

When we give cheerfully and accept gratefully, everyone is blessed.

Maya Angelou

*chapter 3*

# What's in It for Me?

If you're a business owner, you're no doubt one busy individual. Perhaps you just can't see how making space for "giving back" is practical or possible. *My time is far too important to allow for this volunteering of which you speak.* Look, I know that time restraints are real — but giving back doesn't have to mean a trip to Appalachia with Habitat for Humanity. Even if your schedule seems full to the brim, you can probably find one hour a week to make a difference in someone's life. Not to mention that it's a lack mentality (aka poverty mindset) that says, "By giving something to you, I lose something." This may sound counterintuitive, but that kind of thinking is the surest way to keep your sales small and your success limited.

In his foreword to the book, *The Art of Giving*, by Charles Bronfman and Jeffrey R. Solomon, James Wolfensohn describes philanthropy as involving both dreams and plans. He suggests that a philanthropist must be inspired, yet sensible, noting that many people miss the need to do both, instead erring too much to one side or the other. He reinforces the notion that philanthropy begins with each and every one of us — with our dreams, our feelings, our values. And by giving, we become a part of the world at large. By getting involved and taking action, we help others, sure — but we also help ourselves because we benefit from the good we do in the world. In giving to others, we are actually bestowing very generous gifts on ourselves.[4]

If you're looking to create a vibrant business and a vibrant life, practical philanthropy should be an essential component. Giving back can do a few things for business owners. The following are just a few ways you can benefit by becoming a practical philanthropist.

**Helps demonstrate that you're more than just a business owner — you're a human being first.** It's easy to get so wrapped up in our businesses that it can sometimes seem like we need to carve out minutes of each day just to eat, sleep, and spend time with our families. By making a commitment to some level of philanthropy, you have the opportunity to occasionally wear a hat other than that of business owner. This is a great reminder for you, and for the members of your community. And if you choose your cause carefully — getting involved with an organization for which you have true passion — your humanity is sure to shine through.

**Allows you to see others as human, too.** On the flip side, it's easy to become so focused on the bottom line or on networking and business building that we forget that we're doing business with other people. Stepping away from the office to do something not specifically business related — even periodically — will allow you the space to craft very special relationships that might not evolve out of a work environment.

**It makes you feel good.** Have you ever noticed that one of the quickest ways to feel better when you're in a sour mood is by doing something kind for someone else? A friend of mine is a dear woman, but she can be prickly, if not downright caustic on occasion. A couple years ago, she started volunteering with a small nonprofit that helps feed the hungry. She figured she'd go once as a favor to someone, but something interesting happened that day when she gave of herself and allowed herself to be just a little bit vulnerable. She liked it — and she liked the way she felt afterward. So she went back the next week. And the next week. And now, someone who'd never seen the value or importance of volunteering goes every week to help make a difference in the lives of the less fortunate. She's a regular — and she has regular customers, people she actually looks forward to seeing each week. I won't say that she's never ill-tempered anymore, but she's definitely calmer and nicer to be around these days.

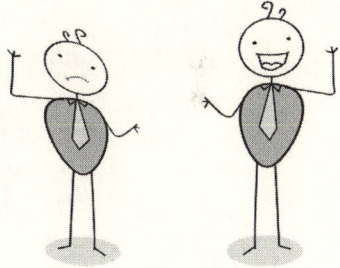

**Offers a way to rally clients/customers and the public around shared passions and goals.** How much is good word-of-mouth advertising worth? Some would say it's priceless. But in order to get the word-of-mouth going, you've got to do something that is "buzz worthy" — something to get people talking about you. Taking an interest in a cause and putting your business name out there when you get involved is a great way to do this. It's even better if the cause is one that your clients/customers are likely to join you in supporting. While it's impossible to guarantee that any single act is going to generate buzz, visibility within your community can only help your business. Your visibility is sure to increase if you can successfully rally your clients/customers and the public to join a cause you believe in.

**Opens doors to valuable and lasting community connections.**
Every nonprofit organization has a board, some of whose membership rosters include the most elite personalities in the community. Depending on where and how you choose to get involved and give back, you may find yourself rubbing elbows with people you might not otherwise have the chance to meet. You already know you share a common interest with them, right? Who knows what kinds of valuable and lasting relationships can come from such shared passions? It could lead to a joint venture or an introduction or the opportunity of a lifetime. One caveat — don't join the organization with the sole aim of meeting a specific individual. These are smart people who can see duplicity coming a mile away; such behavior is not the goal of practical philanthropy and it's likely to backfire anyway.

**Builds trust and customer loyalty.** Much like the idea of being a person first, your philanthropic activities can give your customers/clients reasons to trust you, which in turn will help you build customer loyalty. Depending on the research you read, it costs at least twice as much — some reports indicate six to seven times as much — to acquire a new customer/client than it does to retain an existing one. Trust, loyalty, and a good name are just a few of the things that can result from your practical philanthropy.

**Becomes a part of a company's brand identity.** One of the best examples of this is Toms Shoes. Though the company began with shoes, they've branched out to other areas now. Yet their philosophy remains the same: "With every product you purchase, Toms will help one person in need." In just eight short years, what began as an altruistic startup has managed to donate 10 million pairs of shoes to needy children in more than 60 countries. They built giving into the fabric of their brand. Virtually anyone who knows Toms knows they give shoes to needy kids. How can you make practical philanthropy a part of the way you do business?

**Positions you as a good corporate citizen.** Like the people who comprise them, companies — whether small or large — must live and thrive within the communities, neighborhoods, towns, cities, states, countries, continents, and world around them. Like good human neighbors, good corporate citizens must act responsibly, with honor and integrity, if they desire to stay in business. Involvement with a reputable nonprofit or civic cause can help cement a positive perception of you and your business.[5]

Laura Orsini

There are many reasons to "give back" in both your business and your life. Chances are you will experience many benefits once you become a *practical philanthropist*.

Every episode of the TV show "Undercover Boss" demonstrates poignant examples of corporate philanthropy — many of them quite grand. For those who've never seen the show, presidents, CEOs, and other senior company stakeholders wear disguises as they walk and work among the employees and staff of every kind of major company, from 1-800-Flowers to the Chicago Cubs to Kampgrounds of America (KOA). As regular feature of the show, the "undercover boss" eventually reveals his or her disguise to startled employees. The boss then demonstrates his or her gratitude to their staff by making philanthropic gestures like paying employees' hospital bills, footing their college tuition, paying off mortgages, and more. Some "bosses" make more grandiose gestures than others, but to a person, they "give back."

OK — so you're probably not going to go out and buy your virtual assistant a new Jaguar, but might there be ways you can model the giving-back concept from this wildly successful series on a smaller scale that works for you?

# Review Question

How might *you* benefit from "giving back"?

_____

_____

_____

_____

_____

_____

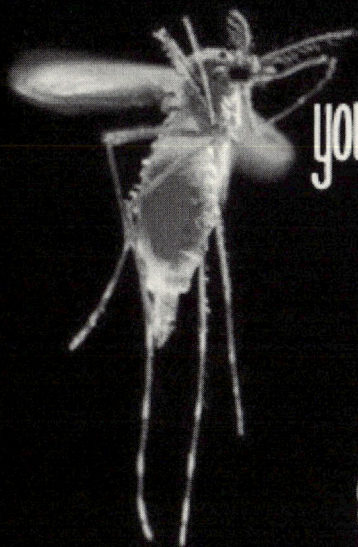

If you think you're too small to make a difference, you've never spent a night in a tent with a mosquito

AFRICAN PROVERB

*chapter 4*

# Can One Person Really Make a Difference?

Perhaps you agree that giving back might be a good idea, but you're wondering, "How much good can a little bit of my help really do?"

Perhaps the most obvious analogy is a candle in a dark room. It's pitch black, no light from any source. You strike a match, and there's light. Use the match to light a candle, and there's sustained light. It might not be bright, but it's definitely no longer dark. Join your candle to another candle, and it's brighter still. Join your candle with many other candles, and the darkness is gone. That's how you can make a difference. Start by lighting one candle.

Human examples are all around us. Warren Redman, a UK psychotherapist and president of the Emotional Fitness Institute, tells the story of a woman who was having a bad morning, but decided to shake off her self-pity by recognizing that although she couldn't change her circumstances, she could change the way she chose to experience them. Her new perspective led her to smile at a stranger, who stopped and engaged her in a conversation. The two spoke for nearly an hour, until the man finally thanked her and went on his way. Two days later, the same man sought out this woman to thank her for saving his life. He explained that he'd been desperate and literally ready to commit suicide when she smiled at him on the street. "It was the first happy human contact I'd felt in weeks," the man explained. "It gave me a reason to change my mind." Something as simple as a smile had a life-altering effect.[6]

In another incident, a mom tells a story about her daughter, who is in kindergarten. There's a blind boy in the girl's class. Not comprehending the concept of blindness, she asked her mother to explain it. The next day when the mom went to pick up her daughter at school, she saw the little girl sitting next to the blind boy, her own eyes closed as she spoke. The boy had a huge grin on his face. "What were you saying to Tommy that made him smile so much?" the woman asked as her daughter buckled her seatbelt. "Oh, I was just describing what trees look like."

From a post on *facebook.com/LotLRescue*:

> A little more than 30 years ago, a teenager named Jadav Payeng began burying seeds along a barren sandbar near his birthplace in northern India's Assam region to grow a refuge for wildlife. Not long after, he decided to dedicate his life to this endeavor, so he moved to the site so he could work full-time creating a lush new forest ecosystem. Incredibly, the spot today hosts a sprawling 1,360 acres of jungle that Payeng planted — single-handedly.

Laura Orsini

A man from India started planting trees when he
was 16 years old. He's now 47 and lives
in his own forest with rhinos, tigers, and elephants.

The following are a few of the many posts I've shared on my personal Facebook page as a reminder to myself and others that making a difference is easier than we think. In fact, you can join nearly 43,000 others who want to make a difference by checking out:

*facebook.com/OnePersonCanMakeADifference*.

**Laura Orsini** shared We Are Humanity's photo.
January 25

Such a cool pay-it-forward moment!

Temperatures are plummeting in Ontario, so a kind soul has been placing these handmade scarfs around the city. 😊

via **Snow Addiction**

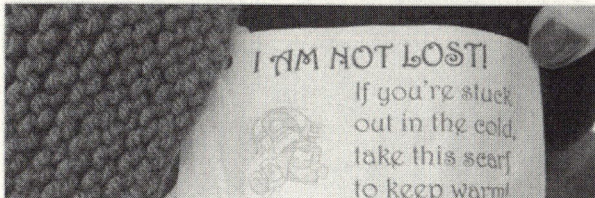

I AM NOT LOST!
If you're stuck out in the cold, take this scarf to keep warm!

Like · Comment · Promote · Share                    👍 22 💬 4

**Laura Orsini** shared One Spark Foundation's photo.
January 27

Gonna keep on sharing the awesome stuff people are doing for each other!

Well One Spark struck again. We were watching this lady when we were at a meeting. We noticed that the tires on her car were the baldest tires we had ever seen. She had to very small kids in the car.

Waited until she went into the dollar gen and we wrote a note and put this on her seat.

Waited until she came out and opened her door and looked into the seat. She opened it up and saw that there was 400.00 dollars and a note that said to get some tires and ice cream. She sat on the seat and cried and then hugged her children.

She then started to do the happy dance. We did not take a picture because we did not want her to know it was us.

PLEASE DONATE TODAY TO HELP US SPARK THE WORLD WITH OUR DOCUMENTARY: http://igg.me/at/1spark/x/6109095 - EVERY DOLLAR COUNTS - WE NEED TO RAISE $57,000.00 BY FEBRUARY 15 ☺

HERE IS AN ANIMATED SHORT DOC TO GO ALONG WITH OUR FILM ☺ - http://www.youtube.com/watch?v=fm8zxsgwZ2o — with LaToya Lawrence-Seltzer.

# Laura Orsini

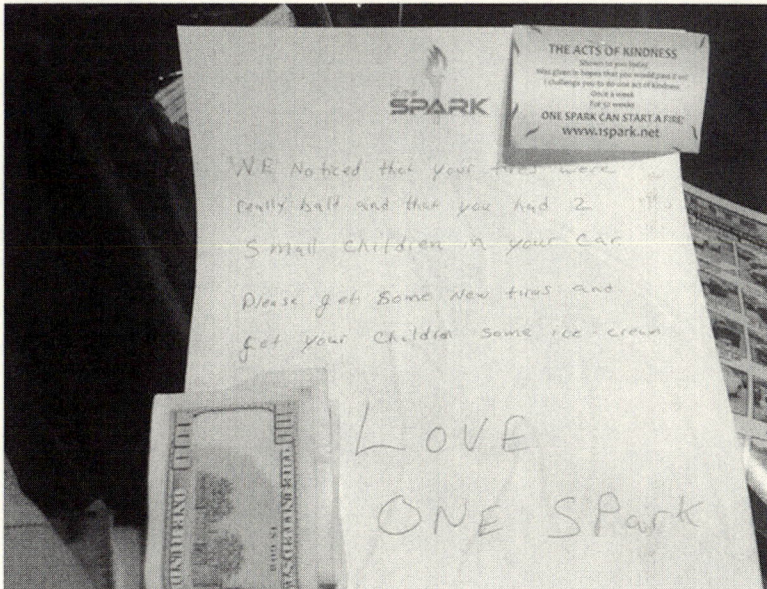

More pay-it-forward awesomeness! It's lovely to share GOOD news.

"Yesterday this pile of blankets was all over the ground filthy, partially wet and frozen having been slept in the night before. I saw a city worker putting the stuff into what looked like a trash can. Then this morning I walk by the same spot and see the blankets had been washed and folded. Made me smile."

Like · Comment · Promote · Share                    14    2

# Review Question

Describe an example from your life of someone who
made a big difference with a small gesture.

_____

_____

_____

_____

_____

_____

tomorrow, smile at a perfect stranger and mean it.

JOHN O'CALLAGHAN

chapter 5

# Where Should I Begin?

I attended a recent networking event that featured a group discussion about marketing. The conversation turned to the idea of partnering with a non-profit as a marketing tool (we'll talk more about this, specifically, in Chapter 6), and one woman asked, "But how would I even know where to begin finding the right nonprofit to partner with?" You may be wondering the same thing. *Who needs my help?*

Begin by examining your passions, interests, and the issues that matter to you. The causes are endless — from suicide prevention to pet rescue to adult literacy to teen pregnancy to drug abuse to environmental concerns to domestic violence to the performing arts to virtually every kind of illness or syndrome. You just need to connect with the one that resonates with you!

Have a cause that no one is servicing? Now I realize this next bit is not for everyone — we are talking about *practical* philanthropy, after all — but you might take a page out of my friend Pam Gaber's book and start your own organization. Pam was like the average American, growing up in a family that was not involved in charitable work. When she made her first forays into volunteering as an adult, it was cautiously and with some serious trepidation.

But like my friend from the earlier story, Pam tried it and she liked it! Soon, her volunteer work with the Phoenix Crisis Nursery led her to introduce her gentle Weimaraner, Gabriel, to a group of frightened, mistrustful, abused, neglected, and abandoned children. It was love at first sight. On just seeing the big gray dog, the children's faces lit up and they calmed down, stopped crying, and ceased fighting (all typical behaviors for children in crisis).

After her serendipitous success, Pam decided to look into volunteering with a pet therapy organization so that she and Gabriel could help more children. There was just one small problem: there were no organizations doing that type of work. So she and Gabriel started visiting the children on their own. Then, a couple friends expressed interest and also began visiting the children with their dogs. These dog-human pairings became *therapy teams*. Soon there were 10 therapy teams, then 12, then 15.

Eventually, without deliberately planning or designing it, Pam became the founder of Gabriel's Angels, a thriving nonprofit organization whose mission is "to deliver healing pet therapy to at-risk children, nurturing their emotional development and enhancing the quality of their lives forever." As of late 2013, Gabriel's Angels had 155 pet therapy teams providing services to more than 115 Arizona agencies and serving 13,000 children annually.

It seems that many nonprofits and service groups start this way. One person sees a need and sets out to meet that need. Their efforts snowball, and without meaning to, they find they've created a movement. Again, starting a whole agency is probably not your goal. But say you work in the computer business. Do you know of an organization that could put old computers to good use? Think about your expertise and circle of incluence. Which alliances you can facilitate? With whom can you partner? Which introductions can you make? Where and how can you get involved? It's probably easier than you think if you just begin looking around.

# Review Question

What are three causes/movements/organizations
about which you are passionate?

1. _____

2. _____

3. _____

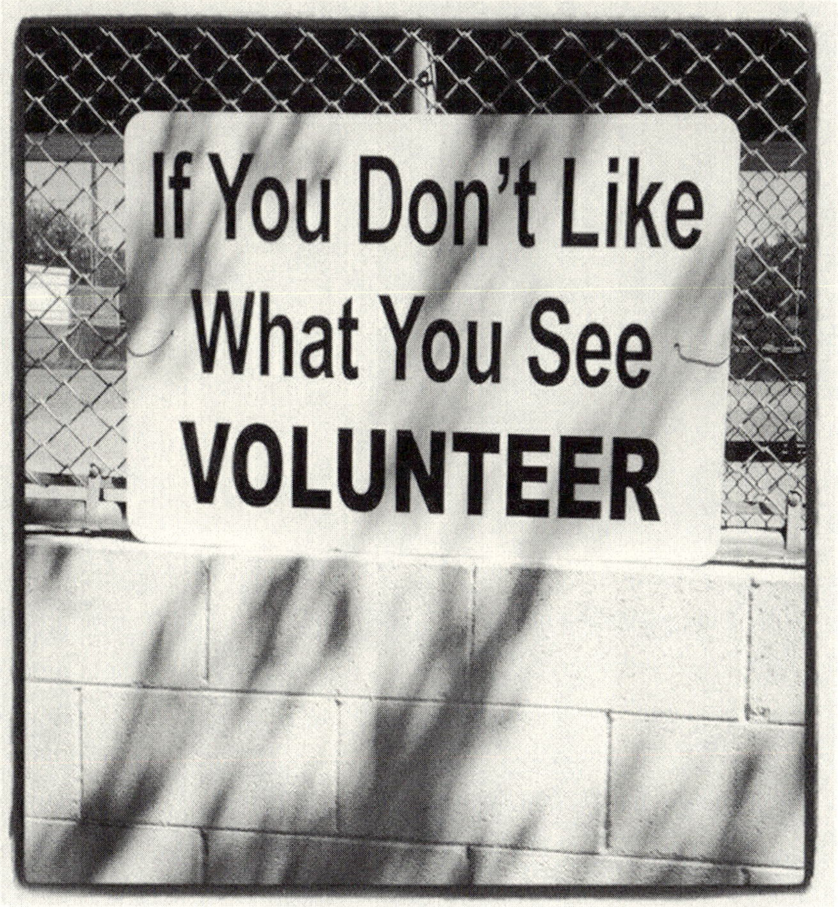
If You Don't Like
What You See
VOLUNTEER

# chapter 6

# Ways to Give Back

As with many things in life, there's certainly no right or wrong answer about how you can or should give back — other than doing something that feeds your soul. If you volunteer just for the PR opportunities or in attempt to win praise, but your heart's not in it, you won't last. It's virtually impossible to remain reliably committed to something we don't value or truly want to do. If you're just stepping your toe in the giving-back water, you might want to start small. There are lots of different ways you can get involved. Following are a few ideas, but this list is in no way comprehensive.

**Volunteer on your own.** *VolunteerMatch.org* is a great site for finding the perfect volunteer opportunity. You can use search fields to narrow down your interests, hours of availability, geographic location, and other details to help you find the organization or opportunity that is right for you. Think the hour or two you donate can't make much of a difference? Think again! The estimated value of volunteer time for 2012 was $22.14 per hour![7]

**Involve your team!** Be a trendsetter and invite your friends, colleagues, clients, vendors, and coworkers to join you in your volunteer endeavors. Doing so gives you a chance to let people know what's important to you and learn more about your values and priorities. This creates great opportunities for initiating and/or deepening business and personal relationships. What kind of activity could you coordinate that matches your company's stated mission?

**Sponsor a food, clothing, or blood drive.** This will take some effort, but it's a great way to share your project with the community. If you have a brick-and-mortar store/office, you can hang a poster or go door to door, asking other businesses to join your drive. Share the love by celebrating the end of the drive with a party; invite your colleagues, clients, vendors, and coworkers.

**Make one of your networking meetings a "giving back" event.**
I'm active with a local chapter of the American Business Women's Associa-

tion, and every year our team chooses a
nonprofit partner. In 2013, we worked
with an organization called the Bridge
Foundation, which works to feed the
homeless in downtown Phoenix. The
group does a great job of providing
sack lunches every Sunday morning,
rain or shine. However, their clients
often ask for things other than food,
like clothing, bedding, and toiletries.

Our group took that information and ran with it, hosting a drive to collect
those items. Instead of our regular December meeting, we got together in
the hall of a church that let us borrow their space to sort and package all
the goods we collected. The next day, a group of us — several husbands
included — got up before the crack of dawn to go downtown to distribute
the goods. It was a wonderful way to network for the holidays outside the
typical luncheon meeting. Do you belong to a networking group that might
try something similar?

**Donate old goods/seconds to a worthy cause.** For example, two of my clients wrote a book about finding one's life purpose. We ordered the first print run and found that the printer had accidentally printed from an old file which still contained a few minor errors. While the clients did not want to sell those books, they decided that instead of throwing them away, they would donate them to a local women's prison — more than likely a win-win, in that the women who received them could probably use the book's info as much as anyone. Do you have old file cabinets, printers, or cell phones sitting around? Do some research! Chances are someone in your area can make use of them.

**Use your social media connections to promote others' events, causes, and drives.** Smart business owners understand the value of social media, but we're not all using it to our greatest capacity. For some, it's a matter of time. For others, it may simply be a matter of awareness. An excellent way to build your own social media following is by becoming known as someone who readily shares information with others. Step up your game by sharing the information your friends, followers, and connections post about their businesses, events, and causes — without waiting to be asked.

**Become a knowledge philanthropist.** Wikihow describes this as a person who wishes to share their knowledge for the benefit of humanity.[8]

An easy way to do this is by posting valuable content on your blog and/or website without worrying that you're "not getting paid" for the information. This is a big one with some folks — the desire to get paid for every single morsel of information they share. Now I'm not suggesting you do complimentary hour-long consultations, publish your books for free, or let people take advantage of you. But I encourage you to get out of the lack mindset that you're giving too much away. Besides, how is anyone supposed to know about your incredible expertise if you're not demonstrating it? Your blog and/or website are excellent ways to do that while you make a difference.

**Create a scholarship fund.** We all know how expensive school is — so without the deep pockets of an "Undercover Boss," what kind of help could we possibly offer? Well, first I encourage you to reframe that sort of thinking. Second, every little bit helps. Virtually any amount is bound to be appreciated by someone. The first thing would be to determine whether you want to start your own fund or piggyback with another group or organization that already has a process in place. If you decide to start your own fund, you'll need to determine the kind of scholarship you want to offer. The more specific you can be, the easier it will be to match your money to the right recipient. Do you want to fund a particular individual, like a single mom, veteran, widow, or high-school dropout who wants to attend a trade school? Or would you like to go more general regarding the recipient, but offering money to attend a specific institution or program? Once you have drafted your parameters, you can begin marketing your scholarship opportunity and looking for applicants. Lastly, you'll need a process by which to determine the scholarship winner(s).

**If you have a storefront, use it to make a statement.** Yes, public political and social statements can affect your business by steering certain folks away; but likewise, they can increase your business by attracting a specific audience in greater numbers. A Phoenix franchise of FastSigns put this sign on the side of their Central Avenue building. What a bold way to make a statement and practice *practical philanthropy*.

**Host an event and donate a portion of the proceeds to your favorite cause.** It could be a bake sale, a casino night, a fashion show, a golf tournament, or anything in between. Think about the kinds of activities that are congruent with your business and your clients' interests. For instance, it might not make a lot of sense to host a skeet shooting tournament if you own a woman's clothing boutique and are partnering with a nonprofit that works to prevent domestic violence. What would you (and your friends, colleagues, clients, and vendors) have fun doing? What kind of event would be easy to pull together? What would yield the most money?

**Become a mentor.** If you had a mentor, you likely know how valuable the process can be. In case after case, mentors claim they get as much out of the mentoring relationship as they give. Mentoring can be a formal process or an informal one. You can do what we all do and hit the Internet, which will no doubt lead you to many mentoring opportunities. Or you might begin instead by asking people you know and trust whether they are mentors and how they met the individuals they are mentoring. People cannot help you unless you let them know what you're up to.

**Give presentations to local business groups, Chambers of Commerce, college classes, or other organizations.** If you're running your own business, you are an expert with knowledge that can help others. A great way to give back is by sharing that knowledge — but it's also a great way to introduce yourself and your business to the wider community. A little leery about speaking in public? Visit *Toast-masters.org* to find a club that fits your schedule and join it. The time and financial investment will pay you back for years to come.

**Use *CrowdsUnite.com* to find a crowd funding platform to help raise funds for your cause.** If you're not familiar crowd funding, hit the Internet, my friend! In brief, crowd funding occurs when many people donate small amounts of money to support a project or cause. KickStarter is one of the most prominent crowd funding sites — but there are hundreds of them from which to choose. As the campaign manager, your primary role will be to create a video explaining your cause and to create and collect "perks." A perk is a gift the donor receives as a "thank you" for their donation. Generally speaking, the bigger the gift, the grander the perk. Social media is a great tool for promoting your crowd funding efforts. You'll probably have greater success if you ask your connections to share your message, rather than asking them to donate, outright.

**Start a Meetup group to help others in your industry.** As you may be gathering by now, giving back can have as many benefits for the giver as it does for the receiver(s), so when the opportunity to give arises, why not take it? Demonstrate expertise in your field by organizing a group where others can get together to problem-solve, network, and share ideas. You nevere know — clients, speaking engagements, joint venture opportunities could come out of your willingness to share what you know.

**Alternatively, scan Meetup for opportunities to join others in making a difference.** Do a keyword search for groups in your area, using terms like "practical philanthropy," "giving back," "volunteering," or "community involvement." Examples include the Spread Kindness Meetup in San Ramon, California, whose members believe in practicing acts of kindness in everyday life. Another is the Cause Marketeers Meetup in Mission Viejo, California, which is a group of business owners with the shared goal of creating financial support for America's charities while improving their own companies' images and increasing their customer bases. One other is the Everyday Utopia Meetup, with groups in Cambridge and Northampton, Massachusetts. These groups of practical idealists get together to share ideas, skills, and resources, to debate, and to collaborate on topics ranging from money to food to ecology to technology and everything in between. There's likely a similar Meetup in your area. If not — you know what's coming next, don't you? — maybe it's time to start your own!

**Adopt a family for the holidays.** This one is obviously seasonal, but a really nice way to extend yourself and your business. If adopting one family is too much for you to do on your own, why not ask a colleague or client to share the project with you?

**Partner with an existing nonprofit.** By now you should have at least an inkling about where your passions and interests lie. Find a nonprofit that could use your business' particular specialization and approach them about becoming a partner. This can take many shapes — including a number of things on this very list. However, by focusing all your attention on one organization, you can gain some valuable exposure for your business.

Benefits of partnering with a nonprofit include:

1. You don't have to reinvent the wheel. Regardless of its size, the nonprofit with whom you are partnering to sponsor activities will probably have a mailing list to whom they will promote those events. And more than likely, they will have a social media presence from which you can benefit, as well.

2. Many nonprofits — particularly the larger ones — have regular conferences, trainings, and workshops. You may be able to leverage your partnership to garner speaking opportunities at their local, regional, and national events. How much would that kind of increased exposure help your business?

3. The people on nonprofit boards have great connections; when you're a partner, as opposed to simply a volunteer, your chances of meeting (or joining) the board increase considerably.

4. They may have a strong relationship with the local media and be able to write and distribute news releases. One of our clients, Jenn Laurent, wrote a book about conscious parenting, *Excerpts From the Heart of a Mom*. In December 2012, Jenn decided to partner with a nonprofit organization that supports abused, neglected, and abandoned kids. The organization sent out its own media release about the partnership, which generated hundreds of inbound links to Jenn's website, something that is vital to the success of the online aspect of any business. She didn't create the partnership with the goal of boosting book sales, but this turned out to be a direct result of her philanthropic actions.

While this list contains many ideas, it is in no way meant to be comprehensive. My hope is that it will inspire you to find a way you can incorporate practical philanthropy into your business' mission and practice. If none of these appeals to you, perhaps one of them will trigger another idea that will work for you and your business.

# Review Questions

Which of your skills, connections, resources, and/or ideas
could you use to begin making a difference for one of your causes?

_____

_____

_____

_____

Which initial steps will you take to begin practicing
*practical philanthropy* (e.g., make a phone call, contact a resource,
engage your team, do some research, schedule a meeting, etc.)?

_____

_____

_____

_____

No one, when he has lit a lamp, puts it in a cellar or under a basket but on a stand, that those who come in may see the light.

Luke 11:33–36

# chapter 7

# Be Sure to Toot Your Own Horn

Chances are, if you're of a certain age — and particularly if you are a woman of a certain age — you were conditioned not to "brag" about your accomplishments. That well-meaning but misguided advice may be the number one thing that has kept women from reaching their potential in busines, and in other areas of life, becuase it perpetuates the mistaken belief that we should keep our accomplishments secret.

When it comes to letting people know about your "giving back," I suggest that you do so fearlessly. A friend of mine, Eileen Proctor, is an expert at generating PR for her businesses. One of the primary ways she does that is by leveraging her philanthropic activities to attract media attention. She has hosted bowlathons for dog rescue groups and acted as MC at fundraisers for organizations like Gabriel's Angels.

Eileen's best advice is this: "Don't do things just to get PR, but when you do things, get PR!" Jenn, my client from the last chapter, did preciselty this with her nonprofit partnership, and it benefitted both her *and* the nonprofit. This is the perfect example of a win-win relationship.

*Practical Philanthropy*

There are many ways you can share the news of your practical philanthropy:

- Talk it up in your newsletter.

- Take photos and/or videos and share them on your social media outlets (e.g., Facebook, Twitter, Pinterest, Instagram, YouTube, and/or tumblr).

- Use free or paid media release services (e.g., ***prlog.org*** and ***prweb.com***, respectively) to send your own news releases about your nonprofit partnerships and successes.

- Write an article about your successful nonprofit partnership and publish it on a site like ***eZineArticles.com***.

- Relate your success stories during presentations or speaking engagements.

- Blog about your practical philanthropy, including links to your nonprofit partners.

- Feature your nonprofit partner(s) on a page on your website.

If you'd like help crafting and submitting a successful media release, please visit my website to download a copy of my free special report, "Media Releases Made Easy" (***writemarketdesign.com/deliver/claim_media_release.htm***).

If you'd like help sussing out a good nonprofit partner or crafting a partnership proposal, please email me at *laura@writemarketdesign.com*. Mention this book in your message to receive a 30 percent discount on our consultation and/or marketing fees.

# Review Questions

To whom will you send your first "giving back" media release?
What would you like this news release to accomplish?

_____

_____

_____

_____

_____

On which topic(s) could you write and publish articles
for *eZineArticles.com* or a similar website?

_____

_____

_____

THE BEST THING
WE CAN DO
IS TO FILL
OUR OWN CUP
FIRST
SO THAT
WE'RE ABLE
TO BE
EXCEPTIONAL
FOR OTHERS.

Gail Lynne Goodwin

# chapter 8

# Thoughts for the "Overgivers"

**DEFINITION OF "GIFT"**

At the beginning of this book, we explored the definition of "practical philanthropy." Now let's take a brief look at the definition of "gift." According to the *American Heritage Dictionary*, a gift is "something that is bestowed voluntarily and without compensation."[9] Webster defines gift as "anything given; anything voluntarily transferred by one person to another without compensation; a present; an offering."[10] The first definition of gift on Vocabulary.com, is "something acquired without compensation."[11] And, according to the online version of *Easton's Bible Dictionary*, a gift is "a gratuity to secure favour, a thank-offering, or a dowry."[12] The common thread among these definitions is the idea of "without compensation." A gift, then, is something offered without any expectation of receiving something in return.

In his book *The Seven Spiritual Laws of Success*, Deepak Chopra touches on the concept of gifting. The Second Law, in fact, is "Bring a gift to everyone you meet."[13] Obviously Chopra is not suggesting that the reader give a physical gift to everyone he or she meets throughout each day (although, a tangible gift is certainly appropriate on occasion). I think, rather, he means to give a greater gift — the gift of ourselves, of our presence — in short, to practice *practical philanthropy*. Such simple yet profound gifts can be offered through a smile, a hello, holding a door for someone, allowing the car in front of us to merge, or sometimes by simply acknowledging the existence of another person. The gift does not have to be big to be powerful. It does not have to be expensive to be appreciated. It simply needs to be given from the heart.

Nevertheless, as we explored in Chapter 3, even the most enlightened and aware of us sometimes catch ourselves thinking the unspoken: *What's in this for me?* Without any malice, we forget to focus on the grace and freedom that come from giving for the sake of giving. This is not a bad thing — it is just us being human. And we do it more often than we may be willing to admit.

I briefly had a roommate in college — because of widely diverse schedules, we never spoke much. In fact, the things I remember about him I can tick off on one hand: His first name was Chris. He spoke fluent Japanese. He taught aerobics, and was on a high-carb diet, eating pasta three meals a day, every day, for all the time I knew him. And I remember his comments about a particular discussion from a philosophy class he was taking at the time. I don't recall the exact context of the discussion — only his remarks about how surprised he was that his entire class and the teacher tore him to shreds for positing that every good act we do in some way benefits us, or we would not do it.

The fact is, Chris' position in that philosophy class all those years ago was correct. We do — and we give — because *we get something in return*. Whether that something is a thank you, a grateful smile, a hug, sex, a reciprocal gift, the assuaging of guilt, or the relief at crossing the receiver's name off a list, in some way, we benefit from the giving.

This somewhat nullifies the conventional "without compensation" definition of *gift*, doesn't it? This is not to say that the giver's getting something out of the act of giving is in any way a bad thing. Just that we do, indeed, get something out of it, or we wouldn't do it. Neither does acknowledging this give-AND-receive aspect of giving in any way detract from or negate the feelings or intentions of the giver. Giving generally benefits both parties — the giver, as well as the receiver.

Sometimes, however, our giving gets out of control.

## WHAT OVERGIVING LOOKS LIKE

During a conversation about practical philanthropy with Elizabeth Hartigan (aka The Gratitude Girl) and members of her Women's Empowerment Circle, the idea of overgiving came up.

While this book was not written for overgivers, it will likely draw their attention, because anything that has to do with giving entices them, exhilarates them, has their name all over it. *Overgiving* means routinely putting others' needs ahead of your own. From your spouse to your children to the PTA to your church to your employer or employees to your political and civic causes to your pets to the homeless guy on the street corner. Someone else (or everyone else) always comes ahead of you, because you feel that doing so feeds you in an important way.

## Practical Philanthropy

A friend of mine explained her experience of overgiving this way:

> For the longest time, I was an overgiver at my church. When I finally quit, I was on 15 different committees. But I didn't look at my invovlement as overgiving. Each time someone would ask me to add another task to my already towering pile, I would say yes, thinking, "I must be very special, because I'm the one they asked to do this." I didn't realize that the only reason they kept asking was because they knew I would keep saying yes.
>
> Eventually, though, I realized that all this giving really wasn't serving me — or my church community. I began to see that if I didn't value myself enough to say no on occasion, even if someone else was "counting on me," no one else was ever going to value me either. Terminating my relationship with the church was one of the most difficult things I ever did in my life, but it was an important step in learning to fill my own cup first so that I'd have something left to give to the others in my life.

Overgiving doesn't have to show up as doing too much; it can also manifest through taking too much ownership for outcomes over which we have no control. One day after months — perhaps even years — of seeing the same homeless man around my neighborhood, I stopped to ask his name. "Curt," he told me. Curt has never asked me for anything. He is always just standing or sitting outside the grocery store, drugstore, or café where my husband and

I frequently eat breakfast on the weekend. Sometimes he has a broom and sweeps up the area. Always he has his bicycle. And never once has he ever been high or drunk when I've seen him.

On the day I asked his name, I also asked Curt if he needed anything. "Well, anything you'd like to give would help, that's for sure," he said. But he wasn't actively begging. He was counting on the good nature of people to offer. Another time, I asked Curt if there was anything specific he'd like to eat. "What would I like?" he asked, almost puzzled, as if answering such a question was beyond his scope of familiarity. "I guess I'd like me some chicken." So I bought him a rotisserie chicken and some fruit that night. I don't always get him food; sometimes I give him a couple bucks. And one night when it was really cold, I gave him one of my husband's flannel work shirts that I found balled up in the backseat of our car.

People don't think of a desert city like Phoenix as getting particularly cold in the winter, but on occasion it does. During a recent winter, we had many nights where the temperatures dipped below freezing. One such night, I was aware that Curt was out there somewhere, and I was heartbroken at the thought of him trying to sleep through the frigid cold. The next day, I told my sister I'd bawled until my eyes hurt at the thought that I couldn't do more to help him. Practical as always, she said, "Yep. That's what happens when you take on a project. You feel responsible for seeing it through to the end." She wasn't saying I shouldn't care — just that when you do care, you often care beyond what you're able to actually do for that other person.

## Practical Philanthropy

Of course, there's also the very real "other side" of the issue, in that the world is, unfortuately, full of scammers and con artists who will gladly take until you have nothing left to give. There's a stretch of road near an Interstate in Phoenix where it sometimes feels like the panhandlers and beggars are piled on top of one another, for blocks on end. I have no doubt that some of these are people who are truly in need, but there are also folks who choose begging as their way of making a living.

Now, I'm neither a shrink nor a spiritual teacher, and this is only *my* opinion, but my first thought is *That's a pretty crappy way to make a living — even if it's by choice.* My second thought is that I wouldn't blame anyone who said, "No way. I can't tell who's really in need, so I'm not giving a cent to any of them."

It comes down to this for me: I've known what it was like to rely on the kindness of strangers. I think most of us have. If we stop helping others because "someone might be taking advantage," we rob ourselves of the chance to make a differnece. I can't tell you what to do: that's why you were gifted with thought and reason and decision-making skills. My preference is to act from love whenever possible — but sometimes that means acting from love for myself and walking away from those who are asking. Not often, but sometimes.

So does my helping Curt out once in a while solve the homeless problem? Of course not. It doesn't even put a dent in it, really. But meeting Curt did humanize the homeless for me in a way that serving meals at the St. Vincent de Paul soup kitchen never did. Those folks were anonymous. Curt has a name and a face, and when I don't see him for a while, I find myself wondering if he's OK. But I also acknowledge that any help I offer him is merely a Band-Aid.

## SIGNS YOU MAY BE AN OVERGIVER

Christine Arylo, of the "Madly in Love With Me" blog, poses a few questions to help you determine whether you may be an overgiver:

- Did you grow up hearing, "It's better to give than receive"? Are you living proof of this in your adulthood?

- Do you value giving and doing more than receiving and resting?

- Is it hard to believe that receiving and resting will give you what you need to be taken care of?

- Have you made yourself "Manager of the Universe?" Does your ego keep you believing that if you don't do it, it likely won't get done or get done correctly?

- Do you believe that you have to give more, buy more, or make more in order to get what you need?[14]

## REASONS WE OVERGIVE

Essentially, our reasons for overgiving boil down to a couple core things: we don't love or value ourselves enough and we feel the only way we can prove our worth is by giving more than anyone else, even if it's to our own detriment.

Author and speaker Jennifer Louden further breaks down our reasons for overgiving into the following bullet points:

- We believe we aren't smart or talented enough to give in the way we really want to give (through our creative work, for example), so we settle instead for pouring out the things we have readily available: advice, money, meals, attention.

- We are afraid to claim what we really want from life, so we distract ourselves by overgiving.

- We were raised in a culture that taught us that we should give until it hurts, give before we take anything for ourselves, etc.

- Women are socialized and innately drawn to be in relationship with others, so we overgive to stay connected to our tribes.

- We're empathetic and have the ability to notice people in need, so naturally we want to help — all of them.

- We want to have an impact and we want our lives to matter.

- We've gotten confused about where giving our best ends and over-providing begins.

- We forget we are human, with humans bodies and human limits.

- We want to be loved, validated, and needed.

- We do it for survival, because we have experienced situations when over-providing kept us from harm.

- We overgive because we haven't yet given ourselves permission to be ourselves.[15]

## HOW TO STOP OVERGIVING

Again, this book was not written for overgivers. But if you see yourself in any of the questions or examples above, it may be time to take stock of your giving and reprioritize your life with *you* at the top! For lifelong overgivers, this is likely much easier said than done. Here are some steps you can take to break the cycle of overgiving:

- **Take that FAA warning to heart:** "Oxygen masks will drop down from above your seat. Place the mask over your mouth and nose and pull the strap to tighten it. If you are traveling with children, make sure that your own mask is on first before helping your children." Realize that it's important, *not selfish*, to take care of yourself first — *before* you start looking around to help others.

- **Write some affirmations and repeat them to yourself daily.** Examples might be:

  *I am enough, just as I am.*

  *I give only as much as I am realistically able.*

  *It's OK to put my needs first.*

  *I value myself.*

  *I love myself.*

- **Learn to accept a compliment graciously.** Don't laugh it off, dismiss it, or play it down. Just say "Thank you."

- **Keep a journal and use it to explore your need to over-give.** Something is obviously in it for you. What is that something? The sooner you can identify it, the sooner you can begin to change it.

- **Ask for support from your friends.** Empower them to remind you if they see you overpromising and/or overcommitting.

- **Do a reality check.** Is it really true that if you don't read every post on your friend's Facebook wall, she will unfriend you? And if she does, was she much of a friend in the first place? Do you truly need the service for which you're bartering, or are you doing it out of some misplaced guilt or obligation? Will your church/PTA/nonprofit group literally screech to a halt if you take a month off from your commitments? It's time to realize that the world is unlikely to end if you begin saying no once in a while.

- **Practice saying "no" without explaining or justifying.** If this is too tough, start with "Let me get back to you," and work your way up to a simple "no." Will it catch people off-guard, especially when they're used to always hearing "Of course!" from you? You bet! Will they ask a second time? Probably. Will they respect you more for standing firm in your "no"? Eventually they will.

- **Stop "shoulding" on yourself and giving yourself unnecessary guilt trips.** A quote often attributed to Eleanor Roosevelt says, "No one can make you feel inferior without your consent." The same is true of guilt. No one can make you feel guilty unless you let them. So stop letting them. And stop feeling guilty for putting yourself first sometimes.

I suggest that any overgiver reading this book begin your steps toward *practical philanthropy* by focusing on *you*.

# Review Questions

Are you an overgiver? If so, what is one way you can begin
reprioritizing your life so that you begin to meet your own needs first?

_____

_____

_____

_____

_____

I hope you have found this book inspirational and/or informative and wish you much success in your journey to become a *practical philanthropist*.

If you are interested in booking me to speak to your company or organization, please email me at ***speaking@writemarketdesign.com***. Mention this book in your message to receive a 30 percent discount on my speaking fees.

Here's to creating a vibrant business — and a vibrant life!

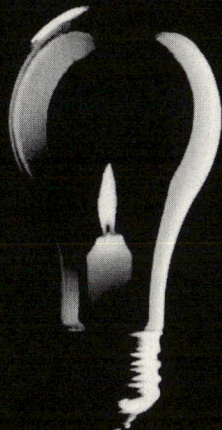

Kindness can transform
someone's dark moment with
a blaze of light. You'll never
know how much your caring
matters. Make a difference
    for another today.

Amy Leigh Mercree

# Share Your Ideas & Success Stories!

Perhaps you've been inspired by the ideas and stories in this book to go out and take up *practical philanthropy* for the first time. Or maybe you've been volunteering and giving back for years. Either way, we want to hear from you!

Please email us and share your success stories. And if you have ideas that would enhance the material here or you noticed something you think we missed (no, we don't claim to be omnicient on this topic, or any other), please let us know.

Reach us:

*practicalphilanthropybook.com*

*practicalphilanthropyblog.com*

*laura@practicalphilanthropybook.com*

*facebook.com/practicalphilanthropybook*

*twitter.com/practphilanth*

CHANGE THE WORLD TODAY.
START WITH THE NEXT
PERSON YOU MEET.

Dillon Burroughs

# Notes

1.  Accessed on 11 January 2014 at http://bit.ly/Pearson_ Philanthropy_Book.

2.  Accessed on 1 October 2013 at http://en.wikipedia.org/wiki/ Philanthropy.

3.  Bureau of Labor Statistics Economic News Release: "Volunteering in the United States, 2012." February 22, 2013. Accessed 1 October 2013 at http://www.bls.gov/news.release/ volun.nr0.htm.

4.  *The Art of Giving*. Charles Bronfman and Jeffrey R. Solomon. Jossey-Bass Publishing. 2009.

5.  Bolded concepts were paraphrased from Entrepreneur.com, "Three Ways to Give Back to Your Community at Holiday Time" by Gail Goodman. Sept. 21, 2011. Accessed 1 October 2013 at http://www.entrepreneur.com/article/220397.

6.  Undated article by Warren Redman on SelfGrowth.com. Accessed on 3 January 2014 at http://www.selfgrowth. com/articles/a_smile_today_could_save_somebody_s_life_ tomorrow.html.

7.  Independent Sector: "Value of Volunteer Time." Accessed 1 October 2013 at http://www.independentsector.org/volunteer_time#sthash.Ll89OAED.dpbs.

8.  "How to Be a Knowledge Philanthropist." Accessed on 3 January 2014 at http://www.wikihow.com/Be-a-Knowledge-Philanthropist.

9.  *American Heritage Dictionary* definition of *gift*. Accessed on 12 February 2014 at http://ahdictionary.com/word/search.html?q=gift.

10. *Merriam-Webster Dictionary* definition of *gift*. Accessed on 12 February 2014 at http://www.merriam-webster.com/dictionary/gift.

11. Vocabulary.com definition of *gift*. Accessed on 12 February 2014 at http://www.vocabulary.com/dictionary/gift.

12. *Easton's Bible Dictionary* definition of *gift*. Accessed 12 February 2014 at http://www.christnotes.org/dictionary.php?dict=ebd&id=1483.

13. *The Seven Spiritual Laws of Success*. Deepak Chopra. New World Library / Amber-Allen Publishing. 1994.

14. Paraphrased from the undated post, "Stop Over-Giving and Over-Doing — start slowing down to receive," by Christine Arylo. Accessed 4 March 2014 at http://madlyinlovewithme.com/stop-over-giving-and-over-doing.

15. Paraphrased from the undated post, "How to Stop the Cycle of Over-Providing," by Jennifer Louden. Accessed 4 March 2014 at http://jenniferlouden.com/how-to-stop-the-cycle-of-over-providing.

PURE LOVE IS A WILLINGNESS TO GIVE WITHOUT ANY THOUGHT OF RECEIVING ANYTHING IN RETURN.

Peace Pilgrim

# Art 4 the Homeless &
# Saint Vincent de Paul

Thank you so much for your purchase! Please know that we will donate 15 percent of the proceeds from your purchase to Art 4 the Homeless, a 501(C)3 nonprofit organization whose mission is to unite all art forms to provide support and awareness of nonprofit U.S. homeless shelters, to provide support for artists involved with Art 4 the Homeless, and to provide a space where artists of all disciplines can create and participate in organizational sponsored activities and programs to raise awareness about homelessness. Find them at *Art4TheHomeless.org*.

We will also donate 15 percent of the proceeds from your purchase to our local branch of the Society of St. Vincent de Paul. SVdP is dedicated to feeding, clothing, housing, and healing individuals and families who have nowhere else to turn for help. Equally important, SVdP provides meaningful opportunities for volunteers to serve their neighbors in need with love and compassion. Learn more at *StVincentDePaul.net*.

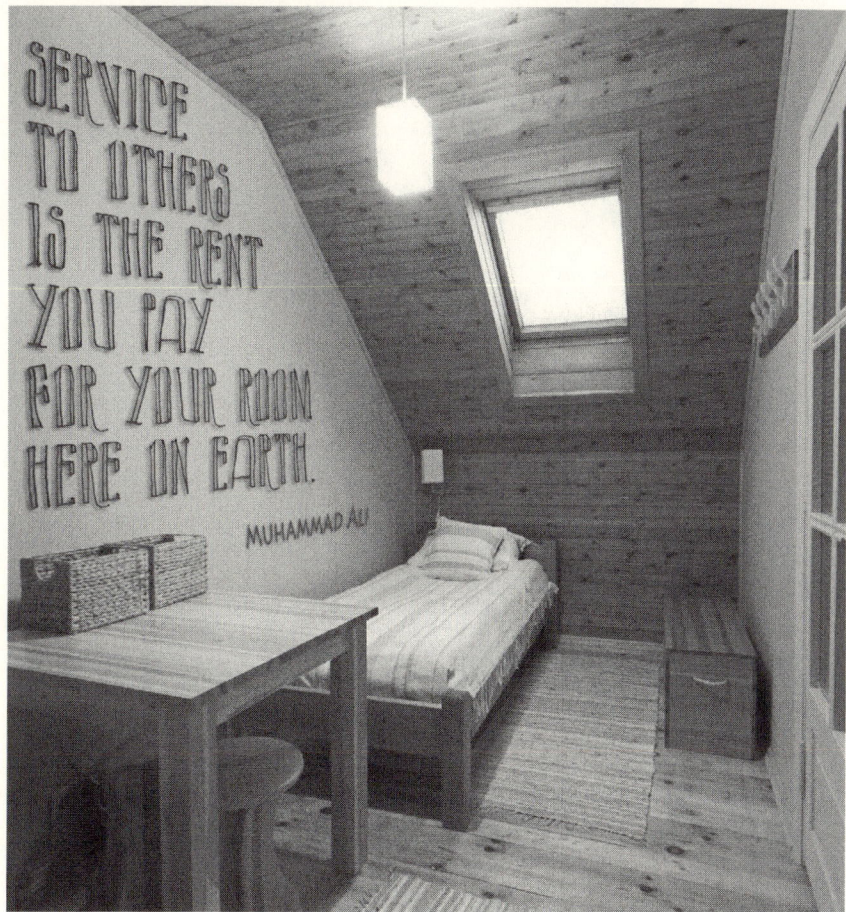

SERVICE TO OTHERS IS THE RENT YOU PAY FOR YOUR ROOM HERE ON EARTH.

MUHAMMAD ALI

# About the Author

**L**aura Orsini is an award-winning author, self-publishing and marketing consultant, and speaker. Her first book, *1,001 Real-Life Questions for Women: A Self-Exploration Experience to Make You Laugh, Cry, Ponder, Ruminate, & Consider* won first place in the Women's Studies category in the 2011 Global eBook Awards. She is nearing completion of her first novel. Laura has come a long way since her first writing award for a Halloween short story in third grade at St. Agnes Catholic School. With a degree in nonfiction writing from the University of Arizona, Laura has a lifelong love of reading, writing, language, and communication.

Laura's personal mission is to empower speakers, coaches, and other change agents to carry their knowledge and passion into the world through their writing. Her goal is to fuel as many people as possible to share their solution-oriented messages — and to dismantle the self-sabotaging belief that they have to be trained writers in order to communicate well. "All you have to do is know (a) what your message is, (b) who your audience is, and (c) why you need to tell your story. The rest — the editing, book production, marketing, etc. — is the easy part. But no one else on earth can replicate the passion and knowledge that you, alone, possess," she explains.

Laura is active in Arizona affiliates of the American Business Women's Association. She also is an accomplished Toastmaster, blogger, and social media specialist. When she's away from the computer, Laura enjoys movies, music, crafting, great conversations, and spending time with her husband and pets.

# Contact the Author

## Laura Orsini — Write | Market | Design

602.518.5376

*Laura@WriteMarketDesign.com*

*WriteMarketDesign.com*

Marcie Brock Book Marketing Maven | BLOG
*MarcieBrockBookMarketingMaven.com*

*Facebook.com/WriteMarketDesign.com*

*Twitter.com/PhxAZLaura*

*LinkedIn.com/in/Laura Orsini*

*YouTube.com/PhxAZLaura*

*Pinterest.com/PhxAZLaura*

*SlideShare.net/PhxAZLaura*

*GPlus.to/PhxAZLaura*

*Quora.com/Laura-Orsini*

*Etsy.com/shop/MoondanzCreationz*